TIME TRAVEL

BY JOHN HAMILTON

Published by ABDO Publishing Company, 4940 Viking Drive, Suite 622, Edina, Minnesota 55435.
Copyright ©2007 by Abdo Consulting Group, Inc. International copyrights reserved in all countries.
No part of this book may be reproduced in any form without written permission from the publisher.
ABDO & Daughters™ is a trademark and logo of ABDO Publishing Company.

Printed in the United States.

Editor: Paul Joseph
Graphic Design: John Hamilton
Cover Design: Neil Klinepier
Cover Illustration: *Spaced Man* ©1979 Don Maitz
Interior Photos and Illustrations: p 1 *Hot Sleep* ©1982 Don Maitz; p 4 *Time Machine* © 1980 Janny Wurts;
p 5 *Spaced Man* ©1979 Don Maitz; p 6 *Back to the Future* poster, courtesy Universal Pictures; p 7 swirling clock,
Corbis; p 8 *Groundhog Day* poster, courtesy Columbia Pictures; p 9 *Timeline* poster, courtesy Paramount Pictures;
p 10 (top) *The Final Countdown* cover, courtesy United Artists; p 10 (bottom) *The Man Who Mastered Time*, Corbis;
p 11 *Light Beam* ©1973 Don Maitz; p 12 *The Time Machine* illustration, Corbis; p 13 H. G. Wells, Corbis; p 14
(top) *The Time Machine* poster, courtesy MGM; p 14 (bottom) scene from *The Time Machine*, courtesy Warner
Bros.; p 15 scene from *The Time Machine*, courtesy Warner Bros.; p 16 person on ladder of time, Corbis; p 17
woman's face and clock gears, Corbis; p 18 people running from giant clock face, Corbis; p 19 *A Sound of Thunder*
poster, courtesy Warner Bros.; p 20 *The Man in the High Castle*, courtesy Putnam; p 21 *Balance of Power* ©1978 Don
Maitz; p 22 Albert Einstein, Corbis; p 23 *Man, Time & Space* ©1976 Don Maitz; p 25 *The Funnel of God*, Corbis;
p 26 clock around Earth, Corbis; p 27 *Light on the Sound* ©1982 Don Maitz; p 28 *The Time Machine; The Anubis
Gates*, courtesy Ace Books; *A Wrinkle in Time*, courtesy Bantam Doubleday Dell; *A Sound of Thunder*, courtesy
HarperCollins; *Timeline*, courtesy Ballantine Books; *The End of Eternity*, courtesy HarperCollins; *The Menace From
Earth*, courtesy Baen Books; *The Best Time Travel Stories of the 20th Century*, courtesy Del Rey; p 29 *The Time Machine*,
courtesy MGM; *The Terminator*, courtesy Orion Pictures Corp.; *Planet of the Apes*, courtesy 20th Century Fox; *Time
Bandits*, courtesy The Criterion Collection; *Timecop*, courtesy MCA/Universal Pictures; *Star Trek IV: The Voyage
Home*, courtesy Paramount Pictures; *Twelve Monkeys*, courtesy Universal Pictures; *Bill & Ted's Excellent Adventure*,
courtesy MGM; *Back to the Future*, courtesy Universal Pictures; *Time After Time*, courtesy Warner Bros.; p 32 scene
from *Back to the Future Part III*, courtesy Universal Pictures.

Library of Congress Cataloging-in-Publication Data

Hamilton, John, 1959-
  Time travel / John Hamilton.
    p. cm. -- (The world of science fiction)
  Includes index.
  ISBN-13: 978-1-59679-996-7
  ISBN-10: 1-59679-996-X
  1. Science fiction, American--History and criticism--Juvenile literature. 2. Science fiction,
English--History and criticism--Juvenile literature. 3. Time travel in literature--Juvenile literature.
4. Science fiction films--History and criticism--Juvenile literature. 5. Time travel--Juvenile
literature. I. Title. II. Series.

PS374.S35H36 2006
813'.0876209--dc22

                              2006012006

CONTENTS

THE SANDS OF TIME

Time travel, more than any other creation of science fiction, is a notion that captures the imagination. It's one of those great "what-if" ideas that launches endless daydreams: what if you could go back in time to meet the heroes and villains of history? What if you knew the Super Bowl scores before they happened? What if you could give advice to your younger self?

Time travel stories are sometimes divided into two categories, or themes: those about the technology of time travel, and those that focus on the *effects* of time travel. The most memorable science fiction tales are those in the second category. For most people, exploring the effects of time travel is the reason we read or watch these kinds of stories in the first place.

In *hard science fiction*, technical explanations of time travel are necessary to satisfy some readers' demands that stories be as realistic as possible. But the fun really begins when characters get to their destination, either in the past or the future. *How* time travel happens isn't entirely necessary to enjoy the story, just like we don't have to know exactly how a ray-gun works to marvel at its power.

Facing page: Spaced Man, by Don Maitz.
Below: Time Machine, by Janny Wurts.

Science fiction is best when it explores different versions of today's reality. When we read stories about aliens, we're really reading stories about ourselves. The same is true of time travel stories. Our fictional heroes go forward or backward in time, exploring cleverly altered realities. In the process, they help us understand the society we live in today.

At their core, however, time travel stories are simply fun, like amusement park rides. Over the years, inventive science fiction authors have dreamed up wild and entertaining plots involving time travel. Some are stories that make you think, like putting together a puzzle. Others have plot twists that make you gasp in surprise. Traveling through time, it turns out, has hidden consequences. There are many ways to mess with the future, or change the past. And when time travelers change the past, they also accidentally alter the present in odd and unpredictable ways.

In the 1985 film, *Back to the Future*, Marty McFly travels to the past in a time machine created by his friend, Doc Brown. The time machine is housed in a specially modified plutonium-powered DeLorean sports car. While stuck in 1955, Marty accidentally interferes with the past. His father fails to meet his mother, which in turn puts Marty's very existence in jeopardy. Marty spends the rest of the movie trying to put things right before he slowly fades away.

Right: A theater lobby poster for Robert Zemeckis' *Back to the Future.* *Facing page:* Traveling through time has hidden consequences.

STEVEN SPIELBERG Presents

BACK TO THE FUTURE

A ROBERT ZEMECKIS Film

He was never in time for his classes...

He wasn't in time for his dinner...

Then one day... he wasn't in his time at all.

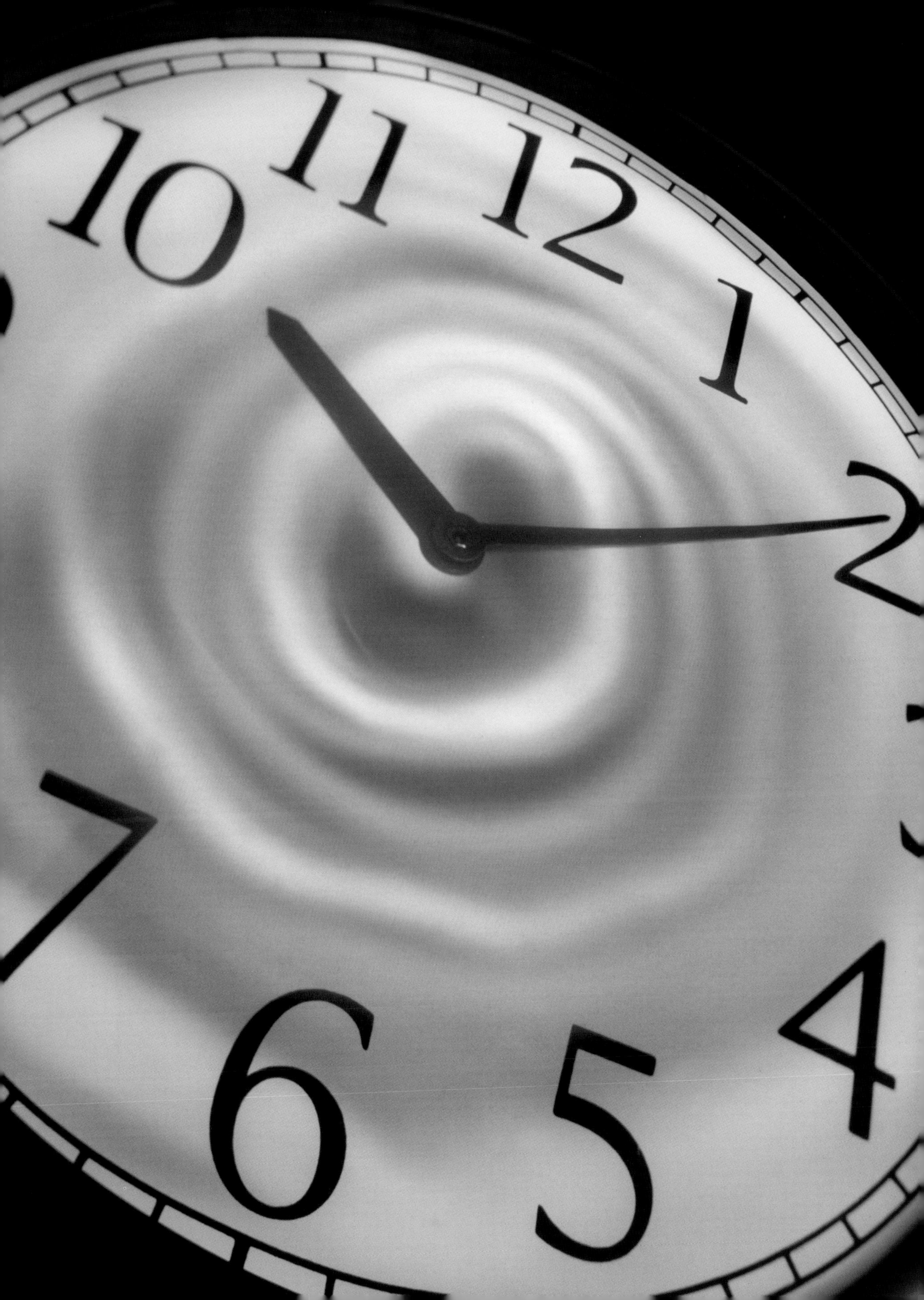

Many non-science fiction stories have characters who travel through time. One example is Mark Twain's *A Connecticut Yankee in King Arthur's Court*, first published in 1889. The hero, a man from Connecticut, gets knocked out in a fistfight, and then suddenly awakes to find himself in Camelot, in the time of the Knights of the Round Table. No real explanation of how the hero went backward in time is given, other than a vague description of the "transmigration of souls" and the "transposition of epochs—and bodies."

Another example is the 1993 film, *Groundhog Day*, which stars Bill Murray as a man who is "doomed to repeat the worst day of his life until he learns to become a better person." It's a great story, and wildly entertaining, but it's not science fiction.

In a true science fiction time travel story, there is at least some sort of science happening, some kind of rational explanation of how people can travel through time. Otherwise, the story is a fantasy. In science fiction, there is often some kind of "time machine," or a scientific breakthrough that allows brave adventurers to travel through time and space.

For example, in Michael Crichton's *Timeline*, a group of historians travels back to the year 1357, to feudal France, where they encounter armored knights, mad lords, and swashbuckling adventure. But unlike *A Connecticut Yankee in King Arthur's Court,* Crichton created a method of time travel that at least seems scientifically plausible, with quantum physics, parallel universes, and the most harrowing use of a fax machine ever devised.

Facing page: A publicity poster for the time-travel comedy, *Groundhog Day,* starring Bill Murray and Andie MacDowell. *Below:* A theater lobby poster for the film version of Michael Crichton's *Timeline.*

FROM THE BEST SELLING AUTHOR OF "JURASSIC PARK" AND THE DIRECTOR OF THE "LETHAL WEAPON" FILMS

TIMELINE

THIS FALL YOU'RE HISTORY

TimelineMovie.com

Above: A DVD cover of the 1980 film, *The Final Countdown.*

This doesn't mean time travel stories have to be realistic to qualify as science fiction. As long as some idea from our natural world, some bit of science, is used to explain time travel, then the story leaves the realm of pure fantasy. But sometimes the "science" in these stories is laughable. In the 1980 film, *The Final Countdown*, a modern aircraft carrier passes through a mysterious electromagnetic storm that somehow transports it to December 6, 1941, the day before the Japanese attack on Pearl Harbor. It's an interesting "what if" situation, based on the thinnest of scientific possibilities.

Right: A poster for Ray Cummings' 1924 novel, *The Man Who Mastered Time.* One of the founding fathers of science fiction's pulp era, Cummings wrote dozens of novels and hundreds of short stories over his lifetime.

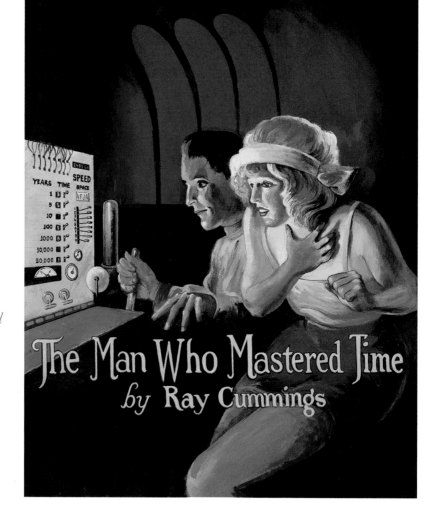

As a matter of fact, most scientists today would argue that *any* time travel story is a fantasy, no matter how much technical language you put into it. While time travel can exist in theory (more on that in a later chapter), actually sending a person through time is an outlandish idea, based on today's understanding of physics.

But that hasn't stopped an army of science fiction authors from coming up with new (and sometimes ridiculous) ways of traveling through time. Instead of pondering the details of theoretical physics, writers are more interested in asking, "what if?" That is, after all, the reason we enjoy science fiction so much.

Below: Light Beam, by Don Maitz.

THE TIME MACHINE

The Time Machine, written by British author H. G. Wells, was first published in 1895. This short book wasn't the first science fiction time travel story, but it was certainly the most important and influential. Writers and filmmakers have been imitating its themes for over a century.

The Time Machine was Wells' first novel. It made him famous, and it remains popular even today. The story's narrator, identified only as the "Time Traveler," creates a time machine made of exotic metals and crystalline bars. Eager to see what the future holds, the time traveler boards his machine. "I drew a breath, set my teeth, gripped the starting lever with both hands, and went off with a thud. The laboratory got hazy and went dark. Mrs. Watchett came in and walked, apparently without seeing me, towards the garden door. I suppose it took her a minute or so to traverse the place, but to me she seemed to shoot across the room like a rocket."

The time traveler increases the speed of his machine until days pass in the blink of an eye. Centuries go by as the landscape changes and evolves. Finally, the time traveler stops. He finds himself thousands of years in the future. It is a peaceful place, almost like paradise. The people who live here are called "Eloi." They are a simple folk, nonviolent, without a care in the world. But their society is built upon a dark secret.

Left: An illustration from *The Time Machine,* showing the time traveler meeting the peaceful Eloi.
Facing page: H. G. Wells.

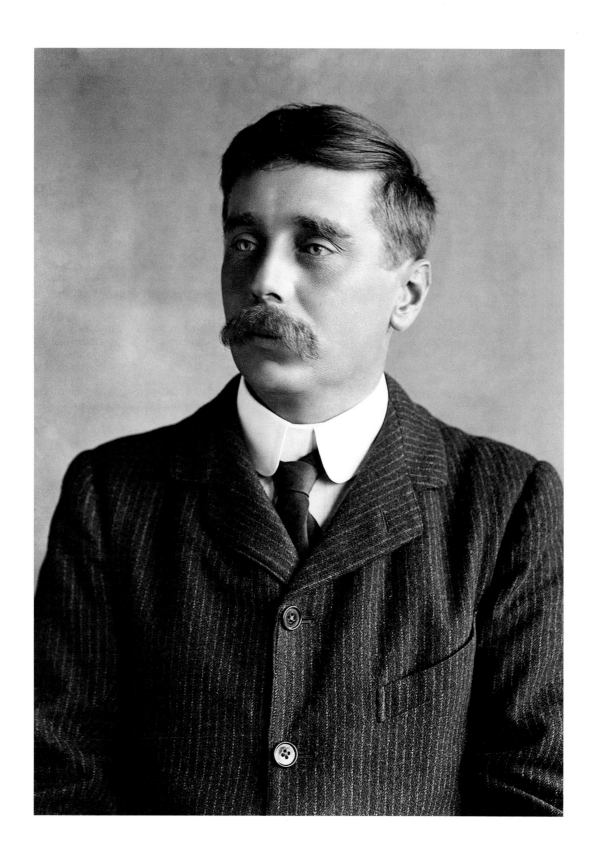

Another race of people, called the Morlocks, live deep underground. The Morlocks provide the Eloi with everything, including food and all the other comforts they need to survive. But on dark nights, the light-sensitive Morlocks emerge to kidnap some of the Eloi and drag them back to their subterranean lair. The Morlocks are cannibals—they harvest the Eloi like cattle.

The time traveler discovers this strange world's sinister side too late: his time

Above: A theater lobby poster for the 1960 film version of H. G. Wells' *The Time Machine.*

machine is dragged underground by the Morlocks. To return to his own time, his only hope is to venture into the Morlocks' lair and somehow retrieve his precious time machine.

After climbing down a long, vertical shaft, the time traveler finds himself in total darkness. He feels soft hands clutching his face. He lights a match and discovers stooping, white creatures with large, fish-like eyes. The Morlocks scurry away from the

Right: The time traveler fights a Morlock in the 2002 film version of *The Time Machine,* starring Guy Pearce.

light, "vanishing into the dark gutters and tunnels, from which their eyes glared at me in the strongest fashion."

With a dwindling supply of matches, the time traveler makes his way through the dark cave of the Morlocks. "Presently the walls fell away from me, and I came to a large open space, and, striking another match, saw that I had entered a vast arched cavern, which stretched into utter darkness beyond the range of my light. ... Great shapes like big machines rose out of the dimness, and cast grotesque black shadows, in which dim spectral Morlocks sheltered from the glare. The place, by the bye, was very stuffy and oppressive, and the faint halitus of freshly shed blood was in the air. ... It was all very indistinct: the heavy smell, the big unmeaning shapes, the obscene figures lurking in the shadows, and only waiting for the darkness to come at me again! Then the match burned down, and stung my fingers, and fell, a wriggling red spot in the blackness."

Above: A Morlock from the 2002 film version of *The Time Machine.*

H. G. Wells was a didactic author; he liked to teach through his writing. He was born and raised in Victorian England, in a society that emphasized the differences between social classes. Lower-class English citizens were often looked down upon, even despised, by people of higher standing.

Through his books, Wells wanted to teach people the evil of this kind of class system. *The Time Machine* is a perfect example. It was a wild adventure story that people loved to read, but it also spoke harsh truths of how class systems can lead to horror and misery.

In addition, naturalist Charles Darwin's theory of evolution was relatively new in the 1890's. *The Time Machine* let Wells, who was interested in biology, explore themes of natural selection, of the strong dominating the weak. By having his hero travel through time, he could show what human society might turn into unless the unjust English class system was changed.

RULES AND PARADOXES

Time travel is one of the most fun categories of science fiction to read or watch. To stay consistent and logical, writers create "rules" for their time-traveling characters. The fun part is then watching how the characters accomplish their goals within these rules, like complicated puzzles being put together.

Because we don't really know what would happen if someone went back in time, writers are free to experiment. Some time travel stories make it clear that you can't change history, no matter how hard you try. For example, a character might try to prevent World War II by killing Adolf Hitler before the war started, but just as the hero is about to pull the trigger of his gun, some other character interferes unexpectedly, or perhaps his gun misfires and he loses his one and only chance.

Another common time travel rule in fiction is that people who go forward or backward in time can observe events, but cannot be seen, or change what is happening. In other stories, the past can indeed be changed, but even the smallest change alters history so much that the time traveler destroys his own future.

Facing page: Time travel stories let us explore what would happen in alternate realities.
Below: A rule in some science fiction stories is that people can observe events, but they can't change the future.

A paradox is an idea that sounds weird or ridiculous at first, but when closely examined seems to actually make sense. Time travel stories are filled with paradoxes. The most famous is the "grandfather paradox." This logic puzzle asks, "if you could travel back in time and prevent your biological grandfather from meeting your grandmother, would you cease to exist?" Of course, if you succeeded, you couldn't have existed in the first place. And since you didn't exist, you couldn't have gone back in time to stop your grandfather from meeting your grandmother. Therefore, your grandfather and grandmother would have met, and you would have been born after all. Mind games like these can give you a headache, but they make time travel stories vastly entertaining.

In science fiction master Ray Bradbury's 1952 short story, *A Sound of Thunder*, a business called Time Safari, Inc. sends customers back 60 million years to hunt dinosaurs. To prevent a time paradox, the hunters are careful to shoot only animals that are already about to die. They also must stay on a special path that hovers above the ground. One hunter, however, strays off the path. When he returns to modern times, the world has changed in many ways. The hunter looks at the bottom of his boot and discovers that he has accidentally crushed a butterfly. This single, tiny mistake has forever changed the future.

Facing page: A theater lobby poster for the 2005 film version of Ray Bradbury's *A Sound of Thunder.*
Below: If you went back in time and prevented your grandparents from meeting, would you cease to exist?

MASTER VISIONARY RAY BRADBURY CREATES A CHILLING FUTURE.

EDWARD
BURNS
CATHERINE
McCORMACK AND
BEN
KINGSLEY

A SOUND OF THUNDER

SOME RULES SHOULD NEVER BE BROKEN.

FRANCHISE PICTURES PRESENTS AN APOLLOMEDIA · QI QUALITY INTERNATIONAL · MFF (SOUND OF THUNDER) LIMITED · FILM GROUP 111 · COCO CO-PRODUCTION IN ASSOCIATION WITH CRUSADER ENTERTAINMENT
A SCENARIO LANE/JERICHO PRODUCTION A PETER HYAMS FILM EDWARD BURNS CATHERINE McCORMACK AND BEN KINGSLEY "A SOUND OF THUNDER" JEMIMA ROOPER DAVID OYELOWO
COSTUME DESIGNER ESTHER WALZ LINE PRODUCER GUY LOUTHAN MUSIC BY NICK GLENNIE SMITH EDITOR SYLVIE LANDRA PRODUCTION DESIGNER RICHARD HOLLAND DIRECTOR OF PHOTOGRAPHY PETER HYAMS CO-PRODUCED BY FRANK HÜBNER AND JAN FANTL
EXECUTIVE PRODUCERS ELIE SAMAHA ROMANA CISAROVA JOHN HARDY RICK NATHANSON JÖRG WESTERKAMP WILLIAM J. IMMERMAN BRECK EISNER
SCREENPLAY BY THOMAS DEAN DONNELLY & JOSHUA OPPENHEIMER AND GREG POIRIER SCREEN STORY BY THOMAS DEAN DONNELLY & JOSHUA OPPENHEIMER BASED UPON THE SHORT STORY BY RAY BRADBURY
PRODUCED BY MOSHE DIAMANT HOWARD BALDWIN KAREN BALDWIN DIRECTED BY PETER HYAMS
WARNER BROS. PICTURES
PG-13 PARENTS STRONGLY CAUTIONED
Some Material May Be Inappropriate for Children Under 13
Sci-Fi Violence, Partial Nudity and Language
www.asoundofthunder.com

19

ALTERNATE HISTORY

"Alternate history" is the name of a very popular variation of the science fiction time travel story. Instead of having heroes travel backward or forward through time, these stories imagine a kind of alternate universe in which major events in world history have somehow turned out differently.

Alternate histories are closely related to time travel stories. Both kinds of fiction allow authors to explore "what if" questions. An alternate history story holds a mirror up to our society by changing reality in some basic way, and then steps back to see what happens.

Facing page: Balance of Power, by Don Maitz.
Below: A paperback book cover of Philip K. Dick's Hugo Award-winning *The Man in the High Castle.*

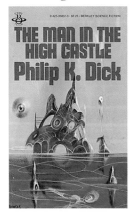

In the 1953 novel, *Bring the Jubilee,* author Ward Moore imagined an America in which the Southern Confederates won the Civil War. Science fiction writer Harry Turtledove revisited that theme in 1992 with *The Guns of the South.* Turtledove has written many alternate history novels, including the *Worldwar* series, in which hostile aliens invade Earth in the middle of World War II.

In 1962, acclaimed science fiction author Philip K. Dick published *The Man in the High Castle.* This important novel takes place 15 years after the United States has lost World War II to Germany and Japan. It is a very character-focused book, despite its larger themes, such as racism, slavery being made legal once again, and Jews being killed by Nazi occupiers. It's a disturbing tale of ordinary people living under the tyranny of foreign armies, and of regaining their lost cultural pride. The book also deals with the shifting nature of reality—what is real, and what is merely illusion? This is a theme that crops up in many of Dick's novels. In 1963, *The Man in the High Castle* won the Hugo Award, science fiction's highest honor.

TIME TRAVEL FOR BEGINNERS

Many scientists no longer believe that time travel is merely a wild science fiction idea. Time travel, at least in theory, is a real possibility, based on our current understanding of physics. If we can somehow harness these theories, it might actually be possible to send someone forward or backward in time. That's an extremely difficult task, however, and won't ever happen with the technology we have today. But perhaps someday, in the far future, an advanced civilization will unlock the secrets of time travel.

Facing page: Man, Time & Space, by Don Maitz. *Below:* Physicist Albert Einstein, in a lighter moment.

Albert Einstein was a physicist who did his most important work in the first half of the 20th century. Many think he was the greatest scientist of all time. His "general" and "special" theories of relativity changed how scientists think of time and space. We understand now that time is a fourth dimension of our universe, along with up-down, left-right, and backward-forward.

Einstein's theories of relativity are a complicated mix of theoretical physics and math. Simply put, Einstein proved that space and time are combined, unified in a single model called the *space-time continuum*. Measuring time depends on the speed of the person observing the clock. To an observer on Earth, when an astronaut's spaceship approaches lightspeed (the fastest anything can go), time seems to slow to a crawl. But to the astronaut, time back on Earth seems to be speeding up, even though the astronaut is aging normally. This affect is called "time dilation." After a very long trip, the astronaut might return to find that everyone he knew on Earth had grown old and died.

Scientists have proved this theory by placing sensitive clocks on the ground and on fast-moving objects such as the Space Shuttle. After landing, the clocks on the Space Shuttle are a few nanoseconds slower than the timers on the ground. Technically, the Space Shuttle astronauts have traveled into the future.

Another important idea (especially when it comes to time travel) is that an object with enough mass can actually "bend" the space-time continuum. Think of a thin rubber sheet stretched out over the head of a drum. If you roll a steel ball over the drum, the rubber will bend downward. The same kind of thing affects space-time. Astronomers have, in fact, seen light rays "bend" around massive objects, such as stars or black holes.

A black hole is a star that has died and caved in upon itself. All of the star's remaining mass is crushed into a super-dense object called a "singularity." It has so much mass that everything, even light, is sucked into its gravity-well.

A black hole that rotates, like our Earth, is called a Kerr hole. Some believe that when an object, such as a spaceship, is sucked into a Kerr hole, it is ejected into another, alternate universe. These alternate universes might be just like ours, only forward or backward in time. The spaceship would be spit out of a "white hole," a kind of exotic matter that behaves the opposite of a black hole. But even if this is possible (and some physicists insist that it's not), how could an astronaut survive the crushing gravity deep inside the black hole/white hole? And even if you survived, how could you ever determine where your ultimate destination was? And how could you safely return?

Facing page: A painting of Earth caught in a black hole, by Albert Nuetzell, for author Robert Bloch's story, *The Funnel of God*.

Unlike black holes, wormholes exist only in theory. But many scientists today are convinced that they do indeed exist. A wormhole is like a tunnel that bridges distant points of the space-time continuum. Think of a large apple. If a worm were to get to the other side, it might crawl all the way around on the skin of the apple. But a smart worm would cut that distance by boring a hole right through the apple. That is how a space wormhole would work.

Remember that Einstein proved that massive objects curve space-time. Wormholes are created by two massive objects, such as black holes, bending space-time in different parts of the universe, so much so that the two depressed ends actually meet. If you built a model of a wormhole, it would look like two mouths on the opposite ends of a long throat.

The great thing about finding and using a wormhole would be jumping to a distant galaxy without having to actually travel the standard distance, which might normally take several lifetimes.

The thought of time travel using a wormhole can be mind-boggling, but try to keep in mind Einstein's theories of time and space. Pretend that scientists have invented a way to create super-massive objects that make wormholes. Imagine a pair of twins: one stays on Earth, and the other travels in a spaceship with a portable wormhole generator, which she'll activate at the end of her journey. The astronaut travels close to the speed of light for several weeks. Because of Einstein's relativity theory, back home on Earth time speeds up much faster than for the astronaut.

The astronaut throws a switch and creates the wormhole, which connects to Earth. Looking through the wormhole, the astronaut can see that her twin is now an old lady. If the astronaut were to step through the wormhole, back to Earth, she would in effect be traveling into the future. At the same time, if the twin on Earth were to step through the wormhole onto the spaceship, she would be traveling into the past!

Wormholes, Kerr holes, and other exotic matter, such as cosmic strings, can be used for time travel—but only in theory. Whether these forces of nature can actually be harnessed and put to practical use is a question to be answered by future scientists—or by the imaginations of science fiction writers today.

Facing page: Light on the Sound, by Don Maitz.
Below: Time travel today exists only in theory—and in the minds of science fiction writers.

27

GREAT TIME TRAVEL STORIES AND MOVIES

TOP TEN BOOKS AND SHORT STORIES

The Time Machine by H. G. Wells (1895); available from Penguin Classics

The Anubis Gates by Tim Powers; Ace Books (1983)

A Wrinkle in Time by Madeleine L'Engle; Bantam Doubleday Dell (1962)

A Sound of Thunder by Ray Bradbury; HarperCollins (1952)

Timeline by Michael Crichton; Ballantine Books (1999)

The End of Eternity by Isaac Asimov; HarperCollins (1955)

By His Bootstraps by Robert Heinlein (1941), available in *The Menace From Earth*, a collection of eight Heinlein short stories; Baen Books (1999).

Time's Arrow by Arthur C. Clarke (1950)*

Death Ship by Richard Matheson (1953)*

Rainbird by R.A. Lafferty (1961)*

* Available in *The Best Time Travel Stories of the 20th Century*; Del Rey (2004)

   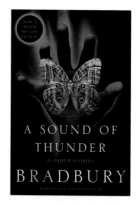

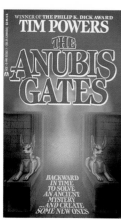 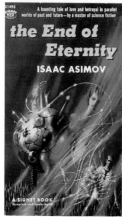  

Top Ten Films

The Time Machine (1960)
The Terminator (1984)
Planet of the Apes (1968)
Time Bandits (1981)
Timecop (1994)
Star Trek IV: The Voyage Home (1986)
Twelve Monkeys (1995)
Bill & Ted's Excellent Adventure (1989)
Back to the Future (1985)
Time After Time (1979)

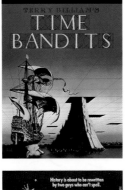

GLOSSARY

DIDACTIC

Intending to teach, especially giving moral instruction. For example, H. G. Wells is often called a didactic writer. His stories are thrilling adventures, but Wells also intended to teach his readers about the hidden dangers of the rapid rise of technology.

FEUDAL

A social system common in medieval Europe (from about 476 A.D. to 1450 A.D.) in which a king granted land to his nobles in exchange for loyalty and military service. The common people, the peasants, in turn lived on their lord's land and gave him loyalty, a share of their produce, and military service when called upon.

GALAXY

A system of millions, or even hundreds of billions, of stars and planets, clustered together in a distinct shape, like a spiral or ellipse. Our Earth is located within the Milky Way Galaxy.

HALITUS

Freshly exhaled breath, often sour-smelling. In *The Time Machine,* when the time traveler said, "... the faint halitus of freshly shed blood was in the air," he meant that he smelled the foul scent of fresh blood.

HARD SCIENCE FICTION

Science fiction that emphasizes facts and reality. Hard science fiction is filled with scientific detail. It tries to present a realistic speculation of how science will affect future societies.

HUGO AWARD

The annual award presented by the World Science Fiction Society to honor the year's best science fiction. The award is named after the legendary writer and editor Hugo Gernsback, who founded *Amazing Stories* (left) in 1926.

KNIGHTS OF THE ROUND TABLE

The legendary group of knights who swore loyalty to King Arthur of Britain and who lived at the castle of Camelot. The Round Table was a large table where many knights could sit together in a circle. In that way, no single knight was more important than another. In addition to King Arthur, some of the most famous knights who sat at the Round Table included Sir Lancelot, Sir Gawain, Sir Gareth, Sir Kay, Sir Bedevere, Sir Bors, and Sir Galahad.

LIGHTSPEED

Light travels at a speed of approximately 186,282 miles per second (299,792 km/sec).

NATURAL SELECTION

A process where organisms that are better able to survive in their environment produce more offspring, ensuring the species' survival. For example, an animal that has a skin that acts as camouflage (perhaps through a genetic mutation), would better be able to avoid predators. This animal would be more likely to survive and then produce offspring that also has camouflage. This process was observed and described by naturalist Charles Darwin, leading to his Theory of Evolution.

PARADOX

A statement or idea that appears at first glance to be absurd or nonsensical. But when closely examined, the paradox actually appears to have some truth to it. For example, the "warrior's paradox" states that the more you train to fight, the less likely you are to actually get into a fight. This makes some sense when you consider that martial artists are trained to recognize dangerous situations and learn to avoid them. Also, bullies and thugs tend not to pick on people who carry themselves with confidence.

QUANTUM PHYSICS

Regular physics (often called Newtonian physics) describes how matter interacts with other matter (gravity, electricity, velocity, etc.). Quantum physics is the study of how these interactions change when observed at the atomic level. In other words, the laws of physics are different—often very strange—when the object you're observing is as small as an atom. Many exciting ideas, including time travel, may become reality by studying quantum physics.

INDEX

Below: A scene from *Back to the Future Part III.*